Drumright's Unique History

by Eileene Huff

Rare Photos of a Boom Town Born
to Survive

NEW FORUMS PRESS INC.

Published in the United States of America
by New Forums Press, Inc.
1018 S. Lewis St.
Stillwater, OK 74074
www.newforums.com

Library of Congress Cataloging-in-Publication Data Pending

This book may be ordered in bulk quantities at discount from
New Forums Press, Inc., P.O. Box 876, Stillwater, OK 74076
[Federal I.D. No. 73 1123239]. Printed in the United States of
America.

International Standard Book Number: 1-58107-096-9

Cover design by Sue Hill.

Contents

Drumright's Unique History

By Eileene Huff

This series of articles published in the *Drumright Gusher* in 1995 was awarded first place in the "Distinguished Service Award For Preservation of State and Local History" by the Oklahoma Heritage Association.

Ceremonies were held during a luncheon in Oklahoma City on January 12, 1996. Jack Graves, President of the Oklahoma Heritage Association, made the presentation.

Preface

It is the- purpose and intention of this book to be a source of learning the facts and human interest sides of a Boom Town that grew despite all odds.

It is intended this book should provide a source of memories for the hundreds of families who lived and were a part of this famous oilfield's unique history.

It is not intended to be a compilation of details and statistics, rather a dedication to the strength, character, innovativeness and determination of this mass of *unmatched personalities* who, each in his own way, made a contribution to the development of the largest oilfield in the world in 1912-1913 and a Boom Town that has survived 92 years.

Eileene Huff
June 8, 2004

"Drumright is the Poster City for Rural America,"
Senator Ted Fisher, Oklahoma Legislator.

"If I could have the vote of every person who ever lived in Drumright, I would get more votes than the Governor."
Lou S. Allard, Jr., on running for Lieutenant Governor of Oklahoma.

Dedication

To my father, Benjamin Franklin Russell, one of Drumright's first photographers who came to Drumright in 1912 and to my mother, Gladys Vergne Bethea Russell.

About the Author

Eileene Russell Coffield-Huff was born in a brown box house half a block north of Broadway on Pennsylvania in Drumright. This had been her father, Ben Russell's Photo Studio during the boom days.

She lived in Drumright all her life, except for the time she was at the University of Oklahoma. At Drumright High School she was one of Orville von Gulker's jornalism students who went to work immediately after graduation.

She was editor of the *Drumright Journal* before she was 20 and has had a career in free lance writing. Her writing focus and speaking opportunities have been primarily on Drumright and Oklahoma.

When this seies of articles "Drumright's Unique History" was published in the *Drumright Gusher* there was an outpouring of requests for copies. That is what justifies this publication. Her explanation was, "That is because so many hundreds of people have lived in Drumright and heard the stories. Now other generations are fascinated with them."

Acknowledgements

Thanks to the Drumright Historical Museum for its research files; D. Earl Newsom's books, *The Glory Days Of A Boom Town* and *Drumright II, A Thousand Memories.*

Also the Ben Russell Photo Collection and the Eileene Coffield Huff Photo Collection and historic files. Map section created by Jo Ann Baugus.

Drumright's Unique History

Tiger Hill

Tiger Hill begins at Way Park.

One of the questions asked often is how Tiger Hill got its name. Drumright could have been called Tiger because Tiger Creek and Tiger School were in existence by the time Drumright was established as a town.

Drumright has the longest uphill, downhill main street in Oklahoma. The third west hump is Tiger Hill. According to D. Earl Newsom in his book, *The Glory Days of a Boomtown*, there was a separate village called Tiger Town and a steep incline they called Tiger Hill. The main street was known as Tiger Creek Avenue.

In 1912-13 William E. Dunn tried to have a post office established here, according to Newsom. Stories have it that a family of Creek Indians by the name of Tiger once lived here before the oil strike.

The nearest post office was Tiger, located about two miles north. The citizens wanted a post office for Drumright, so a few of them moved the Tiger Post Office to what is now Tiger Hill.

Others applied for a post office for Drumright and were granted one. So to settle the dispute, the government decided to open both post offices. The one that could sell the most stamps in 30 days would be the winner.

Naturally, downtown businessmen swarmed the stamp window, buying as much as a year's supply of stamps. The Drumright Post Office won out.

Only the name Tiger Hill remains.

The Hump

The booming oil town of Drumright brought a rash of gamblers, bootleggers and prostitutes. THE HUMP became one of the most notorious dance halls and gambling dens in the southwest. It was operated by a gang called the Big Six.

It was located between Bartlesville Street and Haven Hill Drive just northwest of Howard Huff's home. Its closeness to the Payne County Line made it convenient for patrons and management to make a run for the county line when pressure from Creek County officers forced them to flee.

In D. Earl Newsom's book, *Drumright, The Glory Days of a Boomtown,* The Hump is described as a cluster of buildings. Newsom writes that it was a large building with two smaller buildings in the rear. A bar was in the front area with gambling tables on the sides.

"It had several trap doors," he writes, "so the proprietor could disappear into a basement room."

Two detailed pen and ink sketches of The Hump drawn by artist Pat Conley McCartney appear in the book.

When entertainer Ruby Darby came to The Hump she drew a big crowd. Newsom records that she was the sex symbol of those times and was known to "ball the jack" on a pool table.

A painting of artist James A. Brill's interpretation

of Ruby Darby dancing, hangs in the Entertainment Room at The Drumright Historical Museum.

Although not employed by The Hump, Hookie Miller was one of the most feared men in oil field history. He often sat in the chair on the east wall reserved for the bouncer to help keep order. Newsom says Miller had lost his hand and part of his right arm and had them replaced with a pointed hay fork which he used as a weapon.

The Hump probably operated between 1914-15. By August 1915 a federal grand jury returned indictments against William J. (Bill) Creekmore who had ties to The Hump, Creek County Sheriff Lew Wilder and other area offices. In a surprise raid in September 1916, officers are said to have chopped up fixtures and paraphernalia in the place. Newsom reports The Drumright Derrick headlines read:

"OVER THE HUMP NO MORE NOW."

Taxi drivers had used the slogan, "Over the Hump and Back" to hawk passenger service.

As Newsom quoted the editor: "No longer do the boys greet each other with the familiar salutation, 'Let's go over the hump.'"

Tom Slick
and the
Wheeler #1

Tom Slick had spent everything he had and his investor's money as well, on nine dry holes. He had even been sleeping on the derrick floor. He felt like his career in oil was over.

That was the winter of 1912.

Discouraged and disgusted, he planned to quit the game and was inquiring of his Bristow friends of something where "a man could make a living."

Slick had been wildcatting in eastern Creek County for the past five years. He had decided that if there

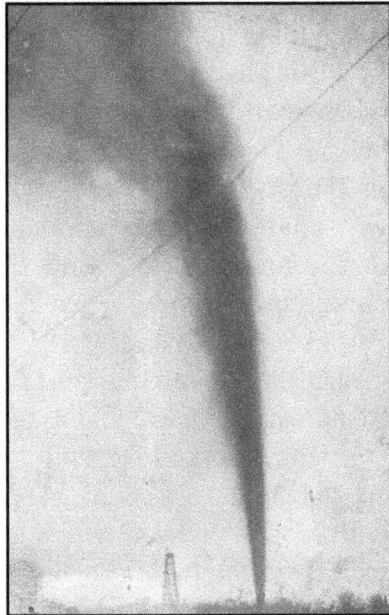

A 6,000 barrel gusher in 1912.

was big oil, it must be in western Creek County. He picked out the Frank Wheeler farm as the spot for the test well.

Late one evening he knocked on the Wheeler's farmhouse door where Wheeler lived with his wife and nine children. They asked him to supper and then to stay the night, which was the custom of the day. When he left the next morning he had a lease in his pocket for Wheeler's 160-acre farm.

He immediately went to Cushing to talk with a group of men who had been investing in oil. But word of his drilling record had reached their ears and they turned him down. The newspapers were referring to him as "Dry Hole Slick" and "Mad Tom Slick."

He borrowed $100, got on the train and went to Chicago to see C. B. Shaffer. Shaffer had just come out of the Pennsylvania oil fields with success and was willing to listen to the proposition.

Slick had worked for Shaffer, so they knew each other. Shaffer recognized that he was a wildcatter, but he also knew he was a competent geologist with a keen nose for oil.

Shaffer liked the idea and gave Slick the $8,000 it took to look at the sand. Back in Oklahoma, the crew dug the hole. When the well came in on St. Patrick's Day, March 17,1912, it roared, spewed and gushed high over the top of the derrick. Slick had found what he was looking for.

They worked fervently to shut the well in and cap it, before word could get out. Slick ordered a fence built around the well with a lock on it. He swore his men to secrecy and ordered them to guard the well with their lives until he got back.

He cut the phone lines at the Wheeler house and jumped in his buckboard. With C. B. Shaffer and lease man, J. K. Gano, they rented every horse, buggy, livery rig in the whole countryside, put them in a pen with guards. He tied up all transportation.

They also sent all notaries on a vacation until they could secure all the leases they wanted.

This blonde, quiet, unmarried, nervous man quickly became the "youngest millionaire in the game." He stayed at the Blue Goose Hotel, not far from the Wheeler well. Now he had a new name, "LUCKY TOM."

But his health was nagging at him. His doctor insisted he remove himself from these intense activities. So Slick took an extended trip to the Orient. He did not get to witness the Drumright field grow derrick by derrick.

When he returned, driving his familiar buckboard, he pulled on the reins, stopped and gazed in amazement at the enormous oil field before him. There were 1,000 oil wells and hundreds of oil tanks and equipment. Unbelievable, even to Slick!

Fourteen wells were drilled on the Wheeler lease. This opened the largest oil field the world had known at that time. Much of what he saw belonged to him, and he was responsible for the rest.

It was Slick who always selected the drilling sites. B. B. Jones of Bristow and C. J. Wrightsman of Tulsa furnished the money. When he left for the Orient they divided their interests. Slick is said to have had 2,500 barrels daily production.

When he died in 1930 at age 47, his holdings were said to be worth $75 million.

(A portrait of Tom Slick and a watercolor painting of The Blue Goose Hotel hang in the Drumright Historical Museum.)

(A special source of information for this column is the copyrighted book, "Drumright! The Glory Days of a Boom Town." *by D. Earl Newsom, used with permission of Evans Publications, Barnsdall, OK.)*

Newcomers Arrive

When the Wheeler # 1 wildcat oil well blew in on St. Patrick's Day 1912, there were only two schools in the area. One had an enrollment of 12 students and the other had 13.

Within 30 days, 300 children had arrived and there was no place to put them.

Oil wells were being drilled so fast and people were coming in at an alarming rate. Every day a robust crew of sinewy men arrived to work the fields bringing their families with them.

Newcomers arrive in Drumright.

Oil companies established quick camps for workers and their families at the site of their operation. But the closest school to many were at least 10 miles away.

Drumright needed overnight help. And that looked impossible.

Aaron Drumright, for whom the town was named, went to Sapulpa to see Fred Patrick, county superintendent of schools. As these two men sat talking, puzzled about how they could accomplish instant schoolrooms, they sighed heavily. Both knew the complications of getting an independent school district and the time it would take to do it. They were aware of the consequences. Without schools mothers and children would leave and fathers would follow, leaving no one to work the wells. Finally, Patrick told Drumright to go back to the oil companies and tell every superintendent to put the teachers on their payrolls. And, he said, don't pay any attention to what anybody says about it. We've got to do it!

So for the next many months every faculty member received a check or voucher showing him or her to be a roustabout, pumper or gauger.

A 100-foot tent was set up on the south side of Broadway and a temporary school was immediately established. Since everything in those days came in wooden boxes, merchants donated 500 wooden boxes and 500 nail kegs for desks and chairs. And school began.

One by one schools began to pop up around the camps. A school had to be close enough for a child to be able to walk. With a field the size of the Drumright oil field and growing, there were many school houses.

Some of the names were Silverdale, Pemeta, Dry

Hill, Tiger, Fairview, Litchfield, Tidal and Pleasant Hill. These were all under the jurisdiction of the Drumright Public School System and called Wing Schools.

Their curriculum provided a child with an education that would be acceptable if he moved to another town.

Some were one room, two rooms. Some had four rooms. All had a basketball court and baseball diamond. They were monitored by a Wing School superintendent. The first was Oliver Akin. He served until he was elected county superintendent of schools and then was succeeded by his wife, Emma. She remained in that position until retirement in 1953.

In 1930, Tidewater Oil Company built the Princess of them all. On the Tidewater Refinery site, south of Drumright, an elegant two story red brick building was erected. It had a bell tower, stage and removable walls that could turn the second story into an auditorium in a flash.

It was not reserved for Tidewater kids alone, any child could attend and more than 20 oil companies were represented.

The wing schools lasted until bussing.

Drumright schools had lots of oil money. Salaries were greater than those paid at the University of Oklahoma. This drew many fine educators to Drumright, which helped establish a strong and lasting educational base.

Wing schools played a vital role in the development of communities for families. With pie suppers, teachers going to homes for Sunday dinners, school programs and holiday celebrations, a special closeness among parents, teachers and children developed.

For some this feeling of warmth, friendliness and caring has lasted a lifetime.

(A special source of information for this column is the copyrighted book, "Drumright! The Glory Days of a Boom Town." by D. Earl Newsom, used with permission of Evans Publications, Barnsdall, OK.)

Boom Town Homes

Women weren't prepared for the houses they would have to live in when they arrived in the early boom days of 1912-1914. Those who came in 1912 were faced with tents for homes.

Later box houses and shotgun houses began to appear. Each looked as its name implies. Box houses were box-like. Shotgun houses were long and narrow with three rooms, a living room, bedroom and kitchen. The name came from someone who said if you stood at the front door with a shotgun and aimed at the back door and fired you wouldn't hit a thing.

These were flimsy, single wall, built-in-a-hurry abodes with little more than a floor, walls and a roof. Old timers described them as being "colder in the

An early Box House in Drumright.

winter and hotter in the summer" than being outside. Ben Russell called his the "Hot Hole."

Many were clustered in the downtown area, but as the town developed and building began, people reached out for the hilly sites to build.

Families sometimes had a struggle fitting into a house, especially if there were several children. The Whorton family who lived on the big boulder back of the present post office, had wooden pegs on the walls where they hung their chairs after supper was over.

The above photo is one of the first box houses. People wanted to send pictures of life in "this new oil country" to their relatives and friends back home. A photographer would take their picture and have post cards made for them.

These post cards played a big role in announcing to the world that there was a huge oil development in Drumright, OK.

Water was available at a city well near the Wheeler #1 oil well site. Women and children would walk daily to the well to bring home buckets of water.

In the Vida Way community near Oilton, Ray Apple told of waiting until his wife had supper on the table in the summertime, then he would run as fast as he could to the community well for a pail of drinking water so it would be cool enough to drink.

Grocers Sam Whitlock and Vier Winans went door to door daily taking grocery orders and delivering them.

Before World War II two large apartment houses, the Broadmore and Broadview, were located side by side in the south bank parking lot on West Broadway. This is where most of the single women school teachers lived.

The Broadview had one long hall with apartments on each side. These were one room efficiencies. The bed folded into the wall. Each had a small bath and tiny kitchen. The kitchen had a small oak ice box with a door on top. A half window-size door in the hall offered the iceman access to the apartment without coming in. He could reach in, lift the top of the ice box cover and place a small block of ice inside. This was a daily procedure.

The Broadmore was larger with two long halls and two room apartments. When the hot weather became unbearable, teachers moved their mattresses to the rooftop and slept there.

During the 1930s depression when a family lost something it rarely could be replaced. The refrigerator was one. It was common to see window-box refrigerators in the north kitchen window of homes. They could be closed-off by pulling down the window. Their efficiency was good only in cold weather.

As for laundry, Mrs. Minnie Tannehill who had five children, washed clothes all day long every Monday. This took place outside if at all possible. Then Tuesday she ironed all day. (Early day washing machines are on display at the Drumright Historical Museum.)

By 1917 some of the finer homes were being built. The P. J. Stephenson home on North Cimarron had one of the first bathtubs. Mr. Stephenson sent his wife, Anna, to Kansas City where she purchased everything to furnish their new home, furniture, dishes, even linens.

Drumright Needed a Library

For the first 20 years of Drumright's life, there was no public library. Several had talked about it including Dr. Dale Warner, a dentist, Katharine (Mrs. Jack) Schickram, former teacher and Drumright High School Journalism and English instructor, Orville Von Gulker.

When the 1930s depression began to dig deep in the minds and souls of the community, a supportive

Drumright Public Library

group decided the need was past discussion. Drumright needed a library now.

Permission was granted to use a room on the second floor of the City Hall. There were lots of shelves, a few books and steep stairs to be climbed to reach it.

Nonetheless, the new library was a success right from the start.

Von Gulker became a forceful voice in trying to secure a building of their own.

Through the efforts of a supportive group, the WPA (Works Progress Administration) approved this impressive structure to be built on the banks of Way Park in the Hollow and construction began.

It was dedicated in 1936 with a lot of fanfare. The native stone building with large arched windows and high pitched roof was the pride of Drumright. The floor plan was almost the same plan as today's library.

The manager of Drumright's theaters and the Drumright Journal offered a "Book Matinee." Every child who brought a storybook received a free pass to the show. This resulted in 500 books piled high in the theater lobby. At the same time kids were learning about the new library.

Then, unexpectedly in 1956, a tornado came rolling fiercely down the Hollow from the southwest, catching the library in its fury, hurling books in every direction and destroying the building.

It was unbelievable how quickly management of the Long Bell Lumber Company on North Ohio offered the lumberyard as a temporary storage. Townsfolk came from everywhere, filled their arms and cars with books and transported them to the new quarters where they remained until the new building was built.

---

by Eileene Huff   17

Old Crow Bridge

Nothing challenged the progress of the oil fields more than "The River." When it was up and out of its banks, crossing was impossible and work came to a halt.

The Drumright Oil Field stretched from Shamrock to near Oilton, where one of the great fields, the Vida Way Lease, was located. Rigs were thick up and down the Cimarron, even in the river bed. Getting materials and equipment to the drilling and production sites had to be done.

People following the oil booms respected the River as well. When A. E. Peck was attracted to the Drumright Boom in 1915, he was living at Avant and

Crossing the Cimarron with a boiler.

chose Oilton for his next home. He tore down his hardware store and funeral parlor and moved the whole thing along with household furnishings by freight train to Jennings. There he arranged to have it ferried across the Cimarron.

Peck got into the funeral business when he lived in Kiefer. Said to be one of the toughest towns in the country, there were lots of shoot-outs and no one to take care of the dead. He hired an undertaker and added a mortuary to his hardware store in an instant.

Until construction of the "Old Crow Bridge" near Oilton, teamsters either ferried or forded the 80-yard span, coaxing the horses, pulling and straining to keep them moving, so as not to bog down and take their cargoes with them. Their loud "Gee-haw's" resounded down the river's bend, as they yanked to avoid known pockets of quick sand.

When it was finished, the Crow Bridge stood as a mighty giant to progress. Only a section of its girders now cling to the bank as a reminder of the past. Its replacement, of concrete and steel, offers a safe, smooth crossover.

The bridge became King of the Oilfield and a hedge against the river's fury. Waters below could no longer detain work and idle the crews.

Soon wagons, heavy with casing, steam boilers and rig timbers rolled onto the wooden bridge floor, shaking, rattling, sometimes swaying under their shifting loads.

Long preparations were made to drill an early day well. Wooden derricks were built by hand and stood 72 feet tall. That is hard to imagine in this day when oilmen can drill and look at an oil sand all in one day.

In 1982 W. J. "Snooky" Taylor and Barry Hubbard built the three story bank at the corner of Broadway and Morrow in Drumright. It was their dream to keep the story of yesterday's oil alive pictorially.

They selected a group of photographs that now hang in the SpiritBank and had them enlarged.

Focus of the graphic art display is the mammoth mural of the Crow Bridge, stretching 54 feet across the south wall of the lobby. The mural arrived in 18 rolls, each measuring 3 by 8 feet. A Stillwater specialist skilled in hanging wall paper was commissioned. He came with paste pots, scaffolding and razor bladed instruments. Working meticulously to avoid a wrinkle, he unrolled the sections, splicing them together until the 8 by 54 foot mural was adhered to place.

The mural has a strange fascination for visitors. The bridge looms in front of you, as if you could step onto its wooden planks and cross the river right there. But walk back and forth and watch the bridge follow, beckoning you. Its mystery is hard to unravel.

The mural hangs today as both a memory and a tribute. The bridge captured the challenge of the river and closed the gap of delay for the robust men who worked the oilfields.

Methodist Build Their Church

With the Wheeler No. 1 wildcat oil well in 1912, Drumright became a Boom Town. Over night there were street fights, shoot-outs, saloons, dancing girls and gambling. Rough, tough and noisy.

By 1913 the editor of the Drumright Derrick ran a story saying that not all people who come to the oilfields are rough and tough.

"Many are refined, educated and progressive," he wrote. "Our lady population is something elegant, ladies of refinement and intelligence."

First Methodist Church Bell Tower under construction, 1914.

He called for all "God Fearing People" to gather at the Air Dome Theatre the following Sunday to organize a Sunday School. The Air Dome was actually an outdoor theatre and boxing arena. More than 700 people came and the Union Church was organized. It was designed for Christians of all denominations.

It wasn't long before many Methodists wanted their own church. Mrs. Dale Schaffer of Cushing led the campaign and money was raised in less than one month to build it.

By the spring of 1914, the First Methodist Episcopal Church of Drumright was dedicated. It was a white frame building located where the present structure stands. M. Jones of Bristow, who had oil interests here, donated a 50-foot lot. Other lots were purchased and a parsonage was built behind the church site.

When the crash of 1929 came, almost on the heels of the completion, this clause saved the church.

This structure served the congregation until the 1920s when membership roles grew to 900. Plans were drawn to build a new church, a beautiful edifice and architect F. A. Duggan, Tulsa, was engaged to design it.

The new $45,000 structure began to rise in the middle of Drumright's business district. The parsonage next door was built at a cost of $4,000.

The building represents the perpendicular period of English Gothic architecture. Exterior walls are Arkansas boulders laid in cement mortar. The tower is 72 feet high. Spires are carved crockets with finials of Bedford Stone and a gargoyle placed on one of the spires.

On dedication day, April 22, 1928, money was raised and pledged to assure liquidation of the $30,000 debt. But the full force of the Great Depression changed everything and it looked for a time that the church might be lost.

However, Mr. Jones' deed saved it and the Methodists sent Rev. J. W. Coontz as pastor to Drumright. Through almost super human efforts and considerable know-how, the church was finally liquidated for about 66 2/3 cents on the dollar.

In his efforts to raise the funds, Rev. Coontz organized a $29,000 club composed of 19 teams with husbands and wives as co-chairpersons. The final payment was made on January 22, 1945.

The church has been a birthplace for many cultural affairs. The Ensemble Club presented four piano recitals here for more than 40 years. Boy Scouts have met here since the church was completed. Ladies of the church has served Rotarians their Friday meal for more than 50 years and it is a voting place on election day.

Red Cross had headquarters here during the 1956 and 1974 tornadoes. About 20 Drumright Nursing Home patients used it for a temporary residence during the 1974 tornado. It became a community kitchen during that same tragedy where 500 to 600 were fed for days.

The church opens its doors to the community on Christmas Eve when they hold a Candlelight Service in a quiet atmosphere of music and worship. Pews are filled with two and three generations of families who have been coming for a quarter of a century. It has become a homecoming.

In 1931 value of the church properties was $31,000. Today they are valued at more than one million.

The church is on the National Register of Historic Places. It stands in tribute to a community that built a city out of a Boom Town.

Vida Way

The oil community of Vida Way just grew without planning. It began after C. B. Shaffer and Tom Slick completed the Wheeler #1 at Drumright. Almost overnight, the oil boom was on and the whole countryside was a noisy, boisterous, hard-working, floating population of so many thousands they couldn't be counted.

While the Drumright field was being developed, oil was discovered along the Cimarron River north toward Oilton. Then they brought in the fabulous well on the Vida M. Way lease, four miles southwest of Oilton and it became a community, mostly out of ne-

600 foot swinging bridge across the Cimarron River near Vida Way.

cessity. The men who worked there had to live in the field.

More than a dozer major oil companies, two gasoline plants, a couple of grocery stores, Vance Chapel and Vida Way School all hugged together in this four square mile boundary to create a community.

At its peak, it said that about 500 people lived here. In the early 1920s, the Cimarron River fields were producing 1,200 to 1,500 barrels of oil per day.

The heartbeat of the community was the four room frame school. Its population was tough, rough and mean. Kids were not interested in learning, they spent their time trying to run the teachers off.

By 1923 there were 175 pupils enrolled. The school board was desperate. The "big boys" would run off a teacher almost as soon as he arrived. The board even hired a woman, but the "big girls" hit her in the head with a baseball bat which prompted her immediate departure.

The school board members learned of a Dean Scott, a principal at Avery and urged him to accept the job as principal at Vida Way. They offered him the regular salary of $55 per month. Scott asked for $60, so they agreed to the split difference of $57.50.

When he arrived at Vida Way, he was immediately invited to a party in his honor. The man, at whose home he was boarding, advised him "to stick an automatic in his pocket and keep shooting until the bullets ran out."

But Scott used another strategy. A gang of bullies crashed the party and didn't recognize the new headmaster. He joined in with them as if he were one of the gang.

Then someone learned he was "packing a pistol" and from that moment things changed. He earned the respect of the students and never once used his gun. He remained there as principal for 16 years until 1939.

The first crisis he had was dealing with the language used by the boys on the playground. They called it "cussin" and they knew the language of the oilfield hands. Every word.

Scott tried several things, but the medicine that cured them was castor oil mixed with quinine. Every time one was caught cussing, he gave him a spoonful, with orders to hold it in his mouth for five minutes.

Scott even opened a night school for ambitious roustabouts, pumpers, drillers and farm bosses with classes held regularly on reading, letter writing and arithmetic.

Soon oil company employees approached Scott to teach them how to make a speech. Most of them admitted to dry tongues and water on the knees when they were called on to speak in a company meeting.

Realizing the importance of this relationship to their jobs, he helped organize the Vida Way Education Club, whose primary function was to practice public speaking.

Scott left Vida Way to accept a job on the Oklahoma Textbook Commission. He became a member of the State Board of Education. Later he was elected to the Oklahoma House of Representatives from Creek County.

Vida Way lasted more than 40 years, when changes of oil field operations made it no longer necessary for workers to live in the field.

First High School

Growth and development of the Drumright schools was as phenomenal as that of the city.

The year (1911) before the Wheeler #1 discovery oil well, 39 students were attending school in this area in a hen house.

By March 1912 after oil was discovered, enrollment jumped to 350 and nowhere to put the students.

Towns people and oil companies viewed this as a major problem. They reasoned that without proper schools, mothers would take the children and leave. Fathers would follow and there would not be enough men to work the oil fields.

Aaron Drumright went to Sapulpa to talk with Fred Patrick, County Superintendent of Schools, to

Drumright High School 1915.

see what could be done. There seemed to be no quick solution. Finally, Patrick told Drumright to tell the company superintendents to put all school personnel on their payrolls until it could be worked out.

For the next several months each received a check or warrant listing him or her as a roustabout, pumper or gauger.

In 1913 there were 600 pupils with nine teachers housed in eight buildings, four in Drumright and four in the oil fields.

By September 1914 more than 1,200 had enrolled. The 1915 enrollment reached the 2,000 mark with a faculty of 31.

The vast oil development gave Drumright plenty of money which attracted qualified educators from over the country.

By the school year 1914-1915, a stone grade building a top a hill at 212 West Federal had been completed at a cost of $35,000. It was called Drumright High School, but grades 1-12 were taught.

In the first graduating class in 1915 were four seniors, three boys and one girl, Clara Spellman Landrum. An alumni association was formed that year and Clara was elected treasurer, an office she held for more than 60 years.

In 1916 a new elegant red brick high school was built at North Pennsylvania and Shaffer (on a hill). The old high school became Second Ward. Its nickname was 'the rock school,' both because it was stone and also because the school yard was peppered with rock outcroppings.

In the 1920s a single oil field pipe fence outlined the school yard. Before classes and at recess it was used as acrobatic bars.

There was a basketball court on the west side of the building.

Both morning and afternoon, when the principal came to the building ringing a triangle, lines formed quickly by classes and children marched into the building to the tune of a Sousa march played on a Victrola that stood in the corner on the first floor.

Three wooden one-room buildings called "overflows" were located on the southeast side of the building to help relieve the heavy enrollment.

There was no lunch program. Sandwiches were brought in lunch boxes or brown sacks. Some ate a hamburger across the street in Mrs. Wade's Kitchen in Mrs. Gibson's (Gibbys) lunchroom.

Sometime after 1929 the gymnasium/auditorium was added and the name was changed to Washington School. With the addition of a new elementary building, Washington was becoming obsolete and soon disbanded as a school.

The Senior Citizens program was initiated here where it remained until this year when it was moved to the Community Center.

Listed on the National Register of Historic Places, it is now private property. Elegant and majestic, it stands as a tribute to the Gift of Education that built a community out of a Ragtown.

Drumright Gets a Bank

Until the Drumright State Bank was established in 1914, most Drumright citizens went to Cushing to do their banking.

In 1914, Aaron Drumright led the way as principal organizer to establish the Drumright State Bank and serve as its first president. The frame building with a screen door was located at 101 East Broadway, on the northwest corner of Broadway and Pennsylvania. It boasted a capitol stock of $20,000 which was printed on the window.

When the new brick building was constructed on this site it was called the Commerce Building. The Drumright State Bank occupied the corner, 101 East

Drumright State Bank which was established in1914.

Broadway. In 1915, the Bumey Brasel Drug Store was established in the east building, 103 East Broadway.

A stairway divided them. Upstairs was the Southwestern Bell Company switchboard for the telephone exchange and an apartment where two of Mr. Brasel's sisters lived.

The bank operated 18 years until August 13, 1932, when just before payday, depositors withdrew such large amounts of cash the bank was unable to meet the demand.

Oklahoma Gas and Electric Company had offices directly across the street, south on the corner. In due time, they moved to the bank's former location, and eventually purchased it.

This building, with its three marble pillar entrance, has been recommended for the National Register of Historic Places.

Brasel Drug had already moved to another location in the 1930's and the Palace Drug Store occupied the building. The store had handsome tile flooring and a beautiful stairway to a balcony at the back of the store.

If proprietors wanted to keep their doors open, flies were a constant problem. So to prevent having to use a screen door, their only choice, they installed ceiling fans in the entry way which served them well.

An early day druggist, E. J. Skidmore, had retired to hunt and enjoy his bird dogs. His favorite dog was named Dan and "Skid" opened a charge account at the Palace Drug Store for Dan.

In the summertime after supper, Dan trotted four blocks from their home on North Morrow, downtown. He turned the corner, headed for the open door and sat down in front of the fountain.

It became a daily ritual. Proprietor Estes Daugherty asked Dan what he wanted and the dog wailed an order, convincing enough to get an ice cream cone which he promptly ate off the floor.

After he cleaned up every crumb, he charged it and went home.

Historic Roberts Hotel and Tower Theater

Drumright's most prestigious block remains only a memory to those who knew it. This historic 100 block on the north side of Broadway was demolished in 1979-1984 to make way for a new bank. In 1916 the Morrow Hotel stood on this spot. When it burned it was replaced by the Roberts Hotel. This four-story brick with a mezzanine was finished in 1918 at a cost of $120,000. Named for Billy Roberts who died

The Tower Theatre and the Roberts Hotel.

before it was completed, the Roberts was a meeting place for oil men, oil deals and traveling salesmen.

It was the pride of the community.

It had the only elevator in town with elevator attendants who made every trip up and down with the guests day and night. There was a cozy coffee shop on the west side of the lobby. Later a full restaurant was opened in front with a street entrance. Once a drug store occupied this same space. The Roberts Hotel had a roof garden, music for Saturday night dances with live bands and later juke boxes which could be heard all over town. The cool rooftop was a welcome retreat from the summer heat. Long dance gowns were the proper attire for ladies.

Many exciting things took place at the Roberts. One prominent Lebanese family prepared for weeks for their son's wedding celebration. Wedding guests practically filled the Roberts Hotel for several days while joining in the festivities. A few couples made the Roberts their permanent residence.

Western Union had its own office on the east side of the lobby, a busy operation with messages in this buzzing community.

Next door on the east was Ernie Morris' Insurance Agency. The back half of this office was occupied by the Harte-Ashwell Dance Studio.

Harry Thomas' Chrysler-Plymouth garage next door on the east had a basement where Harte-Ashwell dancers rehearsed chorus lines all summer for Thursday night park programs.

Next door Howard and Lysle Hand owned and operated a parts store. And then came the Tower Theatre, a first class picture show with air-conditioning, carpeting and first class movies.

The Strand Theater was locally owned until Griffith Enterprises bought the Drumright theatres, remodeled the Strand and named it "The Tower." They operated all three at one time — The Tower, Midwest and Rex.

These movie houses were life savers for the people during the depression. Shows were funny, delightful, musical, warm and compassionate with famous stars playing the leading roles. They let the audience forget everything else for a couple of hours.

The marquee in this photo shows Wallace Berry and Robert Taylor in "Stand Up and Fight."

A boutique owned by Irma Applegate was in the southeast corner of the theatre. Irma was a prominent Drumright shopkeeper for many years, famous for her wide selection of beautiful hats, which she personally selected for her customers.

In the '30s the best place to cool off during the scorching summers was at The Tower. Hot weather started early and kept climbing. In 1936 temperatures locked in at 100 degrees for weeks.

You could walk down to The Tower, stall around out front reading the coming attractions. Ads were decorated with polar bears sitting on blocks of ice. When the swinging doors opened and a rush of cool air came out, you felt like it was right out of Alaska. It only lasted a moment, but you could live with it for a while.

It must have offered more hope than anything else.

A degree of sadness came over the town during the days of the wrecking of the Roberts Hotel. Several Drumrighters purchased chandeliers, staircase railings and other mementos. One man found a 2.5 dollar gold coin in the rubble.

This block was immortalized by Drumright artist, Ronnie Bruce, for the 1994 Oil Patch Jamboree on a T-shirt and pen and ink prints to frame.

Lodges Provide Social Life

Life in the new oil country was fairly isolated. Most of those who worked for oil companies lived at the site of the company office. In most cases it was in the country. The company built rows of small houses that formed a camp where the superintendent, employees and their families lived.

Trips to town were limited, usually for necessities. Other than church, social life was at a low ebb. So it is understandable why secret and benevolent orders became popular in Drumright.

Odd Fellows Lodge and New Post Office in 1916.

Organized in 1913, the first secret lodge was the Owl's Club that boasted of 180 members. Other lodges included AF&AM Lodge No. 468; Knights of Columbus Council 1903; Knights of Pythias, Pythagoras Lodge No. 239; L.O.O.M. (Loyal Order of the Moose); W.O.W. (Woodmen of the World); I.O.O.F. Oilfield Lodge No. 267 (Odd Fellows) and the Masonic Lodge.

Many had companion women's organizations: Eastern Star (Masons), Pythian Sisters (Knights of Pythias) and Rebekahs (Odd Fellows).

Some had their own buildings: The Masonic Temple is located at 219 North Ohio and Knights of Pythias at 138 East Fulkerson. The Odd Fellows Hall pictured above was located across from the present post office on the alley in the 100 block of North hio. A private parking lot now occupies the space.

An early day medical doctor loaned the Odd Fellows $ 10,000 in 1916 to build the two-story brick structure. The lodge hall was upstairs. Ground floor was occupied by the Post Office until the new and present Post Office Building was built in 1940. The Post Office News Stand continued to operate a few years in the old building before it was dismantled.

Construction of the 35 by 100 foot Masonic Temple was financed by the sale of bonds to its members. It was finished in 1922 at a cost of $15,000. Masons have maintained a steady membership and contribute generously to the community programs.

In 1913 two business men, Randel and Winans, built a two-story grocery store west of the water tank. The 24 by 50 foot building's upper story was to be a lodge room where secret orders could assemble.

The Dokey-Moose Club Room was open every day from 9 a.m. until 12 midnight where "all

Dokey-Moose and Knights of Pythias were welcome."

The lodges had kitchens, meeting rooms and a large room for their rituals. The KP building had a dance floor upstairs and members had an orchestra in 1922. When this two-story concrete building was sold this month, the piano was still on the orchestra stage. The ground floor has had several tenants in the past 40 years: McCall & Sebastian Contractors, Turnbow Trailers, Condor Customs and McGuire Salvage Grocery storage.

Most lodges were known for their benevolent work. The Pythian Sisters, Arria Temple No. 4, was organized in 1918 and sponsored the first Girl Scout Program organized in Drumright.

The Masonic Lodge had two youth organizations, Demolays for boys and Rainbows for girls. Both had large memberships and active agendas during the 1930s and '40s. Rainbows extended their activities into the 1960's.

During many years of service with Betty Fisher as Mother Advisor and Past Worthy Grand Matron of the State of Oklahoma, a number of Drumright Rainbow girls were named to "Grand" positions, a state held honor.

Dress of fashion set Rainbows apart from other organizations. Floor length formals, receptions and gifts created a special bond among its members.

Their teachings and principles are structured with fine principles for living and growing.

Many of the outstanding social events in the past in Drumright for teenagers have been the Rainbow-Demolay receptions and dances.

A Saturday Night Town

Drumright was a Saturday town.

If you had a job in the 1930s and '40s, you worked long, long hours, six sometimes seven days a week.

But Saturday was special. This was the day to get a haircut, go to a movie, shop for groceries, furniture or clothes. This was the day to take music lessons, go to the dentist or go to town to visit.

The whistle was on top of City Hall. The head jailer blew it at 12 noon and at 6 p.m. on weekdays.

"Under construction" - Corner of Broadway and Pennsylvania in 1918.

On Saturdays the 6 o'clock whistle was skipped and it was blown at 9 p.m. This announced to shop-keepers it was time to close up and go home.

Drug stores and picture shows continued to be open and Dr. Howard Martin was in his office seeing patients.

His office was upstairs in this brick building on the southwest corner of Broadway and Pennsylvania. He had a small four-bed hospital in the south end of the building and a 60 foot reception room in the north end with doors leading into the small offices on the east side. Straight back chairs were lined around the walls for waiting patients. On Saturday night the reception room was always full.

People would come in from the oil camps early, go to the show and then upstairs to Dr. Martin's. He came to the office about 4 p.m. and stayed until he had seen every patient, sometimes past midnight.

Downstairs on the front was Gene O'Dell's Furniture Store. The two small offices on Pennsylvania were occupied by the law firm of Kermit Nash and Leonard May. Georgia DeBow's Beauty Shop was the farthest south rental.

Car agencies stayed open every evening and long hours on Saturday. There was lots to do in town on Saturday night.

The Tower, Midwest and Rex Theatres ran matinees and evening shows. The Tower was carpeted, air cooled and had a cry room for babies upstairs. Ushers directed you to your seat with flashlight beams on the floor to show you the way.

Popcorn was sold out of Mr. Bundy's Popcorn wagon on the northeast corner of Broadway and Pennsylvania by the OG&E office. Nat's Hot Tamale wagon was across the street west where he lifted the steaming lid and wrapped the delicacies in newspapers, all so hot you could hardly carry them.

Cars parked up and down Broadway on each side and right down the middle as well. It was not uncommon to bring your car to town in the afternoon, park it and walk home. Then after supper the whole family came back to town and the car became visiting headquarters.

People would walk up and down Broadway, window shopping and looking for friends.

You could treat yourself to a triple dip ice cream cone. It was designed horizontally with three cone heads on a single cone stem. Each was filled with a scoop of vanilla, chocolate and strawberry.

Teenage boys hung around the four-corners of Broadway and Penn, standing or sitting on the curbs watching the girls go by.

On special Saturdays there were live models in the store windows. Miller's Hardware and Furniture had drawings in their showroom at the back of the store on Broadway and Virginia. Lots of prizes were given away to customers.

When the 9 o'clock whistle blew, merchants pulled down the shade on the front door, turned out the lights and went home.

The rest of Saturday night belonged to the drug stores, theatres with a midnight preview and the Legion Hut on East Fulkerson, if Bob Wills and the Texas Playboys were in town.

The Railroad Station

People have warm feelings for depots, even after they cease to serve as railroad stations.

The Santa Fe played an important role in the glorious days of Drumright's oil boom with the first passenger train in 1915. Passenger service ended in 1946, but freight was trucked from Cushing and delivered from this depot until 1964.

Santa Fe officials decided to tear down the building, but the Drumright Chamber of Commerce, under the leadership of its president, James L. Shanks, made a strong move to save it.

The Santa Fe Depot

In the early 1960s Drumright was undergoing a change. Young people had the idea that Drumright was dying a slow death. They were going to college and not coming home.

The Delphian Club was an old established study group of women that met once a month to review books. They were concerned about this exodus. Their president, retired educator, Emma Akin, led many discussions about how to change the image of Drumright.

They knew how unique and fascinating Drumright's history is, and conceived the idea of a collection of artifacts in a building that would awaken pride in community heritage.

They decided to develop a historical society and create a museum. The Santa Fe Depot, desolate and run down as it was, seemed to be the ideal location.

But others wanted it as well, such plans for a Teen Town, Food Market, Freight Storage even Junk Storage were their competition.

But this little band of women never faltered . They went to the city commission with their idea, but one member was so opposed to the idea, he vowed right then they would never get it.

Nonetheless, the Drumright Community Historical Society was formed with 128 members and plans continued. The Society sent four men and four women back to the commission with plans and promises. They took a letter from noted educator and former Drumrighter, James A. Brill, who promised to have murals painted on the museum walls if permission would be granted. Two Garden Clubs offered to keep the lawn beautiful with flowers.

This convinced the city to form term lease with

the society on September 10, 1965 and renovation of the landmark began.

But the end was not in sight. Financing became a big issue. The group had vowed never to solicit funds, ever, from anyone. So they interested organizations all over town to have money-raisers. But this did not generate enough money.

The merchants were beginning to believe this museum project would be a mistake and that the organization would become a burden on the community.

Then, the idea of an annual Arts & Crafts Festival, like the one in War Eagle, AR, was suggested. The group went to Arkansas to study their show and held their first Festival in the Masonic Temple.

The community began to fall behind the society. The vision of a museum became a reality.

In June 1965 the Drumright Historical Museum was dedicated. Six hundred patrons were there to join in the festivities. More than 50,000 persons have visited the museum since that day.

The Delphian Club had begun this project as a challenge to enter the Sears and Roebuck and General Federation of Women's Club's contest to try to win the $10,000 prize for the city that would come up with the best project involving the entire community.

They didn't win. But Drumright received a gift of a museum, now recognized as one of the better hands-on small museums in America that tells how, when and why it all happened.

What a record, of how life was, is stored here, since the Wheeler No. I Discovery Oil Well in 1912 that opened the largest oilfield the world had ever known at that time.

So many people have worked here during its 83 years, the continuous parade of former residents returning home is unbelievable.

The museum is their memory in action.

Aaron Drumright House

The Aaron Drumright house at 403 South Creek sits on the south "tip of the hollow," a stretch of hollowed land between two hills that reaches toward Way Park downtown.

It covers almost half a block and has been the home of several prominent families. It was built circa 1914-15 by Dr. Charles Edgar Kahle, an M.D. who came to Drumright in 1913 during the oil boom. He was lured here from West Virginia by his brother, Harry Kahle who was president and director of the Oklahoma Cotton Gin Society.

The Aaron Drumright house at 403 South Creek.

Immediately upon arriving, he plunged into civic work to help Drumright grow and develop. He sponsored the first airplane to visit Creek County. His son, Keith, later became founder and president of Central Airlines and is now in the Oklahoma Aviation Hall of Fame.

He brought Jack Dempsey for a fight and helped arrange an exhibition baseball game with Shamrock on October 25, 1922 and invited Babe Ruth to spotlight it.

That was the day the bases were loaded and the Babe struck out. But the crowd forgave him with lots of applause. Mrs. Kahle invited him to have dinner with them that evening. She served Southern Fried Chicken. It was obvious he had never tasted such a delicious dish. "He couldn't get enough," Keith recalls. "And he ate right down to Mama's platter."

When Dr. Kahle selected the spot to build his home, he ordered all materials from "somewhere in the east." They included pre-cut walls, doors, floors and trim. All were shipped to Drumright via the Santa Fe Railroad and assembled on the site. This is thought to be the first house of this type built in Creek County. But it is not known for sure whether it was a mail-order Sears and Roebuck house.

During the dreadful Flu Epidemic of 1918, Keith remembers his father and his nurse, Audrey, driving from oil camp to oil camp night and day tending the sick for weeks. Keith thought the car was either a Bealie or a Ford. Audrey later became a victim of the flu and died.

Dr. Kahle helped start the hospital on the second floor of the building at the corner of Broadway and Virginia. It had eight or nine rooms.

The family had an Airedale dog named Laddie Boy while they lived at 403 South Creek. It was a full brother to one owned by the President of the United States.

Dr. Kahle's office was upstairs over Skidmore's Drug Store, located at 114 East Broadway on the south side of Broadway.

Laddie Boy became quite ill and Dr. Kahle asked "Skid" for professional advice on how to treat the dog. Skidmore loved dogs, owned fine hunting dogs and doctored many of his own.

His remedy was to chop onions, put them in a clean sock and hold it a few inches from Laddie's nose, night and day.

Neighborhood children became so concerned, they volunteered to take turns helping nurse in relays. They held the onion bag over Laddie's nose through the night and all day long for four or five days.

But all was for nil. Laddie died and the neighborhood children nearly died with him, Keith remembers.

When Mrs. Kahle died of cancer, the family moved to Norman and later to Oklahoma City. A few years ago Keith brought a large collection of his father's medical books and presented them to the Drumright Public Library.

Aaron Drumright, for whom the town was named, bought the house at 403 South Creek.

Way Park Amphitheater

Programs at Way Park during the great depression provided a healing process for people of this area. At the same time it became a cradle for cultural growth that followed.

All this began as a dream in 1931 of Dr. Dale Warner, a dentist. Fifty percent of Drumright's population was out of work with more than 900 heads of households on relief.

Day after day Dr. Warner watched the people with long, sorrowful faces. There were no smiles. If they could only laugh once in a while, he thought, surely they can survive these miserable and frightening times.

He conceived the idea of weekly variety shows. They would be designed like old time vaudeville. When he presented it to the Chamber of Commerce, they turned their heads in disbelief.

Drumright Amphitheater in Way Park.

The next year he presented the idea again and agreed to assume all responsibility for its success or failure.

Fred Way, for whom Way Park is named, was the president and urged Dr. Warner to put his idea into action. Lou Allard, Jr., newspaperman and Arnold Scheer, businessman, were summoned to help plan and stage the programs. This became part of the success of it all.

All shows were on Thursday nights and an audience of 200 or less were expected. What a surprise. There were dozens more than that. They all sat on the grassy slopes. The next week merchants were asked to donate $2 for a board, and volunteers built benches for 600.

In 1936 the present stage was built through WPA programs. When a Drumright committee was summoned to Oklahoma City for planning, they were asked how strong to construct the stage.

"Strong enough for an elephant act!" they said.

The stage was built. There were dressing rooms below and storage rooms for a piano and sound equipment. Two Drumright men created the sound equipment that sent the loud music and laughter through three amplifiers on the stage roof.

And the seating grew to accommodate a crowd of 1,500.

But that count was short. For a few years the audience numbered between four and five thousand people sitting, standing, listening, laughing and applauding.

Alene Harte and Fernette Ashwell, traveling vaudeville troupers, left the circuit, bought a home on

North Cimarron and opened a dance studio. Their students performed year after year.

A scrapbook recording this story along with photos, posters and costumes are on display in the Entertainment Room at the Drumright Historical Museum.

Performers were local talent. Others were professionals sponsored by oil and utility companies.

The Summer Park Programs lasted 25 years. No one ever anticipated that. All shows were free. No entertainer was ever paid.

During the lifetime of the Park Programs in Way Park Amphitheater, shows consisted of almost every conceivable type of variety act.

Except elephants.

Catholic Church and Mosiac Madonna

The Roman Catholic Church was one of the first churches to come to the oilfields. First services were held November 13, 1913, in the Idle Hour Theatre.

By 1914 Drumright had built its first school on West Federal and services were moved to the two story stone school. This was the High School, later Second Ward and finally Washington School.

The mural, Madonna of the Streets, outside St. Mary's Catholic Church.

Three years later, in 1917, the Township of Drumright donated a parcel of land across the street west from the school, on South Cimarron and West Wood, as a site for St. Mary's Catholic Church, where it stands today.

Completed in 1918, it became a mission of Chandler and mass was said every other Sunday. Catechism was held every Saturday morning.

Father William Trienenkens, originally from Belgium, served the church from 1913-1924. His name is on one of the stained glass windows. At his death in 1924, he left $1,500 to the church. The Sacristy was added with the money gift.

Since roads were poor and transportation slow, members built a bed into the wall of the Sacristy to provide a place for the priest to sleep when he came to Drumright. St. Mary's has never had its own priest and has shared with Bristow and Cushing.

Aaron Drumright, for whom the town is named, was a Methodist. His wife, Mary, belonged to the Catholic Church. When she died in 1922, Aaron Drumright presented the first church bell to the parish. It is still here, cracked now and no longer in use.

A building to serve as the first Parish Hall was purchased from an oil company and moved to the west side of the church. When the depression became great in 1931, oil man Henry Becker paid off the mortgage for the hall.

The church had bought an organ, but had not completed payment for it. Becker's daughter, who sang in the choir, donated money to clear the debt. The organ is still in the choir loft, having long outlived its musical life. It has been replaced with an organ located on the sanctuary floor.

About three years ago the Mosaic Mural, Madonna of the Streets, was added to the front of the Parish Hall. Designed and planned on a computer, artist Herb Robb and Father Tim Daley led the parishioners in creating this work of art.

Robb and Father Daley were in accord as to their belief in the relationship between faith and art. They believed sincerely that art helps people to appreciate their world and their faith. They believe it has a certain healing process.

Colors were logged a square foot at a time. Log sheets were given to the workers, who assembled the tiles like a puzzle in square foot sections. All of the work was done by members of the Drumright church. Each person gave more than 200 hours to the project. The hall was literally transformed into a mural-making factory.

Some 14,000 one-inch tiles were mounted one by one. Joe Salem directed the building of the cinder block wall for the art piece. It is trimmed in brick to match the church and Parish Hall.

Upon completion, more than 150 persons from across the state were invited to share in the unveiling and elaborate dedication dinner. Among them was Bishop E. Beltran.

If you get too close to the Madonna you cannot see her face at all. As with all art, it is necessary to study it from a distance.

This Drumright landmark is cared for lovingly by its members. Ninety-nine percent of the things needed for the church are donated by the parishioners. They work hard to keep it beautiful.

The St. Mary's Catholic Church is 77 years old, still in much of its original state. Old Timers will recognize quickly that the church has scarcely changed, just continuously enhanced.

Family Living

Neighborhoods began to grow after the boom. The town was divided into four quarters with Pennsylvania and Broadway as boundaries. Each section had its own elementary school. Because of transportation limitations most of the living and schooling was in your neighborhood.

Women and children rarely rode in a car in the 1920s except on Sunday afternoon when the family took a drive in the country.

One area that developed quickly was the South Jones-Bristow-Creek streets in the southwestern section of the city.

During the 1930s there were 63 children in the four block area of South Bristow. They were in and

A Sunday ride in the country.

out of most houses on that street on a daily basis. Especially in the summertime. Your parents reared you, but the neighbors helped.

With no air-conditioning, windows were up and sometimes it seemed as if everyone lived in one house. Most houses had porches where kids congregated to play, teenagers to date, women to embroider and mend.

Driveways became promenades for "dressed up ladies" pushing doll buggies. These were drag tracks for scooters and roller skates, and on occasions for bounding balls against the house.

There was never a lack of something to do. Children created most of it themselves. The year soap box derbies gained nationwide attention, every overall mechanic in the neighborhood hammered and wired together a soap box car.

Sam Denyer's driveway in the 300 block of South Bristow was the designated testing ground. It was downhill all the way. A sentry was posted in the middle of the street to holler out, "All Clear," signaling the driver to bolt down the concrete strip, sail across the street, pick up Delbert McKensie's driveway right on the finish line. The real skill was to slow it down before the car hit the garage and have shoe leather left.

Houses on the west side had a tier of front steps that served as bleachers. The gallery watched marble games, jack tournaments. Sometimes aspiring actors imitated Bullfrog Charlie who entertained occasionally at the Thursday Night Park Programs. Some of the boys brought snakes from Coal Creek to make the girls squeal.

The tennis court in the 100 block of South Bristow belonged to the W. E. Nicodemous family whose house and yard took up half a block. Mr. "Nick"

---

was the mayor. A group of boys who lived in the Tiger Hill area called themselves the "Tiger Hill Toughs." They hung out there, kept the clay court rolled as smooth as pie crust. Tennis matches were going on continuously.

A five foot lattice fence surrounded the court with one gate near the house. To get over the fence you had to wedge your toe between the wooden strips and vault it.

Up and down Bristow were badminton courts in several yards. Anyone could play. No invitation was needed. The Russell kids built a six-hole miniature golf course in their backyard and agreed to eat pork and beans for six days to get enough cans to make the hole-cups.

During the long hot summer nights families moved to the back yards. Army cots were everywhere.

Those who didn't like the morning sun gathered up their quilts and went inside about 5:30 a.m. Others strung up cotton blankets on the clothes line for sun shades.

Despite the worry that no one could every find you if you stayed in Drumright with no chance to leave this tiny oil town to spread your wings, some went to college, some to war, some to work and became doctors, lawyers, merchants and corporate chiefs. A number of Drumrighters have made remarkable strides in the world.

Two of them were from this neighborhood, Everett Drumright had an outstanding diplomatic career as ambassador to China and Keith Kahle became president and owner of Central Airlines and a member of the Oklahoma Aviation Hall of Fame.

Talent and Culture

It was Tom Fields, editor of the Drumright Derrick, who first said publicly in 1913 that all people who come to the oilfields are not rough and tough.

Mingled with the throngs who poured into town daily was a large group of educated, refined, civic-minded citizens. Many have given Drumright a memorable legacy of the arts.

Especially music.

In the 1920s James A. Brill, art and music teacher at Drumright High School, entered the girl's quartet in state competition and won first. This resulted in a singing tour on the Santa Fe Railway from Drumright to California, entertaining in the Harvey Houses along the way.

Brill, Dr. Dale Warner and Cecil Hinds wrote a musical play, "The Perfume Princess," that was produced in 1926 to help purchase the Steinway Grand Piano that graced the school auditorium for 65 years.

In 1940 two piano teachers, Mrs. A. C. Wiemer and Mrs. Earl Sowers, wanted to try something spectacular and challenging. They invited 22 Drumright housewives to perform in an 11 piano recital. The high school stage was extended to make room for the mass of pianos trucked here from Tulsa.

Out of that concert grew the Drumright Ensemble Club that presented four-piano recitals each spring for some 45 years. Each month, in the early years, the club selected a hymn and asked that it be sung in every church in Drumright during that period, thus bringing the churches in unity in song.

Music has served as a special glue, united the community and serving as a catalyst during bumpy and rocky financial times. Never was it more exhibi-

Julius Budowsky singing operatic arias while cooking Lions Club flapjacks in the 1950s.

ted than when Ronald E. Gerard came to Drumright as school band director. That was 1932. In five years his profound teaching philosophy had the whole town thinking music. When the band played, there was always a crowd. When they paraded, it was as if it were before dignitaries.

The band was worthy of this admiration. Gerard's 70 piece red and white band in 1937 won first place in a state Lions Club contest and a chance to compete in the International Lions Club contest in Chicago in July that year.

The whole of Drumright swelled with pride and vowed to make it happen even though the depression was steadily smothering the community.

Tide Water Oil Co. and the Lions Club sponsored the trip. Three buses chartered and bannered, "1937 Tydol-Veedol Musical Caravan," toured 30 cities in two weeks. The repetoire those teen musicians played raised eyebrows in awe of other high school band directors.

The band became a pinup poster for Drumright. Even today, after 60 years, those who saw them march or heard them play say they can get goose pimples thinking about it.

Jayne Russell, the 17 year old drum major, whose prancing, high-stepping strut set a parade atmosphere on fire. Her commanding baton and distinctive whistle were the overture to the strut. At Chicago she won first, the band a commendable sixth.

Drumright has had many soloists, quartets and singing groups. Frances Tuck Sellers and Julius Budowsky were in demand to sing Jeanene McDonald and Nelson Eddy love songs.

The high school Ten Tones have created lively vocal entertainment under the direction of Luann Branch for the past 25 years.

The Boomtown Theater players create delightful tunes and humorous renditions for packed houses year after year. For 40 years Helen Howard Jones has warmed the hollow banquet halls, churches and theaters with her marimba magic.

Drumrighters are big fans. They endear themselves to those performers who warm their hearts. Whenever there is a musical event in Drumright, there is rarely an empty seat in the house.

Its healing and bonding qualities leave a good taste in your mouth.

(Band uniforms and "The Perfume Princess" manuscript are on display at the Drumright Historical Museum.)

Jeanette, the Talking Parrot

Jeanette was a talking parrot who had been given to Ed L. Thomas by friends in Guatemala. Thomas owned the City Drug Store at 151 East Broadway.

Since the store was open more hours than it was closed, Jeanette lived in the drug store. She had a cage, but seldom stayed in it. She had free run of the store, pacing the long ledges, greeting customers from aloft.

She liked loud talking women who laughed a lot. She loved joining in the conversation with her standard greeting, "What cha doin'?" then mocked them when they giggled.

Even though customers knew that a parrot repeats words mechanically, her voice was so commanding they didn't trust Jeanette.

A regular customer came in one evening and began talking to her. She im-

Jeanette the talking parrot.

mediately descended from her perch, approached him and bent her head as if to bite his hand.

"Don't bite me, Jeanette!" he said.

To which she responded loudly, "I will."

"No you won't," he said as he grabbed his package and left.

She had a keen sense of timing. When a newcomer approached Jeanette, dozing on her perch, and asked, "Can that parrot talk?" she would interject impudently, "I doubt it."

She could imitate almost any voice around her, a girlish giggle, a teenage shriek, soft chuckle or a deep laugh. If a baby cried, she could do that, too.

On Saturday evenings a small band of Salvation Army workers marched from the Citadel and set up their "boiling pot" on the sidewalk in front of the drug store. For half an hour they played their tambourines and sang with hopes of saving a few souls.

When Jeanette heard the tambourines coming, she could hardly get to the front fast enough, squeeze through a small hole and out onto the marquee. Here she paraded back and forth during the entire "meeting." When they sang and preached, she joined in. Her squawking and croaking became such a mockery, people gathered to watch and smile. But the faithful band of worshipers never faltered. "Shushing her" only increased her enthusiasm. Besides it was often evident that Jeanette "kept their pot boiling."

Thomas knew Jeanette could talk. He had heard her in Guatemala. But for months after coming to Drumright she said nothing. No coaxing could change her mood.

One afternoon a Mexican came into the store. When he saw the parrot, he asked if she could talk.

The pharmacist-manager, Billie House, explained she never had since she had come to America.

He began to speak to her in Spanish. At the sound of the familiar words, she twisted her green feathered neck, cocked her head, listening. For the first time, she left the ledge, walked up his arm and sat on his shoulder. She bent her head until her beak was in his face.

He sang a little Spanish song and in a moment she was singing with him.

From then on, her homesickness was apparently cured. She began to pick up English phrases and joined in the merriment of her new home and new acquaintances.

Her laughter was so spontaneous and infectious she was called the "Queen of Laughter." It lasted through the Great Depression and all through World War II. Soldiers often wrote from far away posts to inquire about her.

Jeanette's picture hangs in the Drumright Historical Museum.

Cable Tool Rig

What was a Cable Tool Rig? What did it look like - this rig used to drill hundreds of wells in the Drumright Field, the rig that provided a secure avenue for tools to find the oil sand.

Rig Builders built them by hand, for each well. They were working giants, standing 72 feet tall that literally shook the ground when the crew hit pay dirt.

The oil and gas deep in the Earth roared, gurgled, spewed, then with a wild rushing sound the oil flowed like a rampaging geyser, rocketing over the top and cascading back like a skyrocket.

It was a comedy in triumph as the crew spun their hats into the oily spray, shouting, yelling, dancing in victory.

When the big, thousands-of-barrel-a-day oil wells came in, the burning desire of the ambitious was to get rich quick, to put down another well here and now. It was like a wild, raging, contagious fever.

Young enthusiastic photographers climbed to the top of the rig taking panoramas to print on postcards that would announce to the world the news of the big oil strike in Drumright, Oklahoma.

At night a single electric wire with dangling light bulbs strung to the top of the crown block, then catty-cornered to the power house and beyond to the boiler lit up the sky like a brilliant carnival.

THE CREW, big fat, long lean, handsome, ugly, quiet, boisterous called Big Steve, Slim, Lucky, Moose, Shorty. They liked a laugh, a prank, a chew of Mail Pouch, a drink, payday, a night in town with a bunk in a Cot House for 25 cents.

These were big men with big appetites, who carried enough food for two meals, maybe three, in a bulky aluminum dinner bucket with a bail for a handle. They worked 12 hour tours, seven days a week and never heard of a holiday.

The cable crew was composed of a driller and tool dresser with a drilling superintendent to answer to. The driller was responsible for the well. He was the Skipper. With his hand on the drilling line he could "feel the pulse of the well."

By clutching the taut cable and following it up and down, up and down, he knew what was going on deep in the

A Cable Tool Rig and Flowing Well.

earth. The action of the "jaws" on the end of the drill stem told him whether the tools were stuck, hanging free or hitting bottom.

He diagnosed his own case, used his knowledge and experience to solve the problem. It was his skill that cased off water, his keen perception that kept the drilling bits directed properly to cut the hole.

He made dozens of decisions that belonged only to him and his Cable Tool Rig.

Yesterday the Cable Tool Rig was King of the Oilfield. Today it is a sleeping giant, dwarfed in size and operation by the power tools of the rotary rigs.

The driller, in his new world of geological charts, electric logs, massive equipment still mans the operation. But he no longer takes his signals from the feel of the drill line.

The Cable Tool Rig remains a powerful pioneer, a monument to a giant operation that transformed a frontier into cities and carved a civilization out of a wilderness.

(A replica of a cable tool rig, the dinner buckets and a pair of driller's shoes are on display at the Drumright Historical Museum.)

Tour Historic Boomtown U S A

1. The Hump
   103 South Bartlesville
2. Longest Uphill-Downhill Main Street in Oklahoma
   Broadway City Limits East to West
3. 9 Places on the National Register of Historic Places
   A. Aaron Drumright – 403 South Creek
   B. J. W. Fulkerson-508 East Broadway
   C. Drumright Historical Museum—Broadway & Harley
   D. First United Methodist church—115 North Pennsylvania
   E. Washington School (site)—212 West Federal
   F. Wheeler #1 Oil Well—North Harley
   G. Tidal School (now Winery)-2 miles south Highway 16
   H. Drumright Gasoline Plant #2 (site)-1.5 miles north on Highway 99
   I. Jackson Barnett #11 (site) 1.5 miles south on Highway 16
4. Row of Shotgun Houses–100 Block East Drumright
5. Boomtown Theater—Live stage performances– Downtown Drumright
6. "The Cimarron" (Bigger than Southfork)–Lou S. Allard Drive-South
7. Aaron Drumright Home (Babe Ruth ate fried chicken here)–403 South Creek
8. World Famous Tiger Hill–West of Pennsylvania & Broadway intersection

BoomTown
Locations

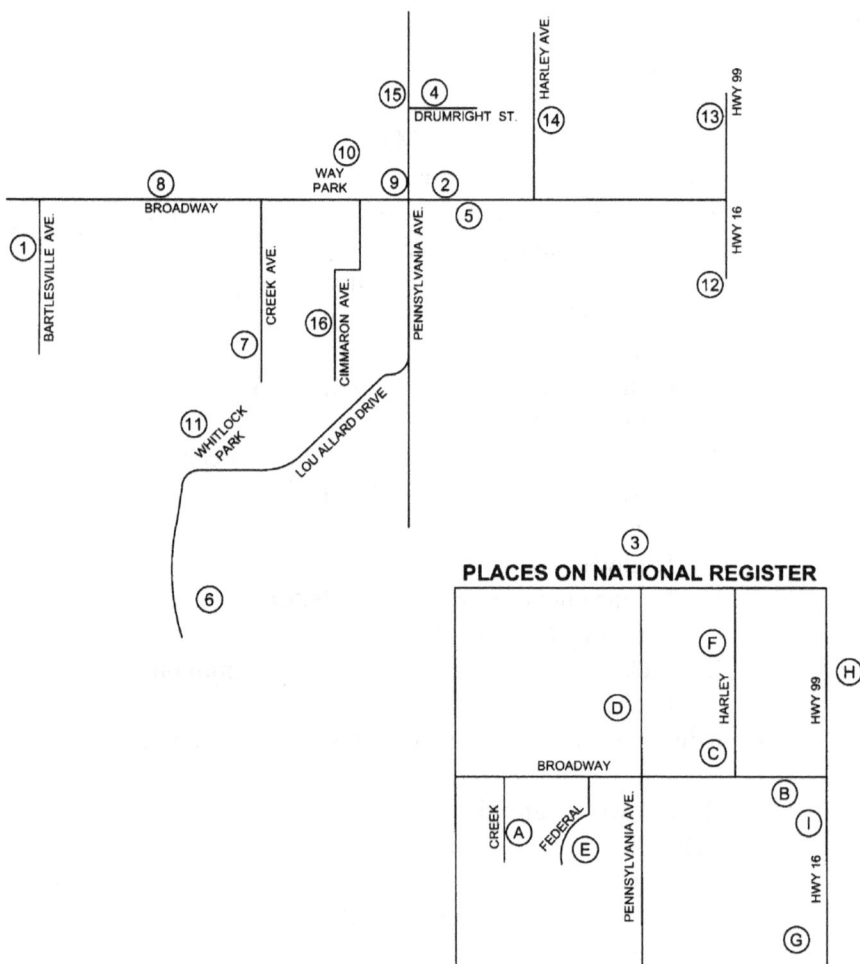

9. 54 foot mural of "Crow Bridge" on the Cimarron River (It follows you as you walk)–SpiritBank–25 West Broadway
10. Downtown Way Park–between Morrow and Cimarron on Broadway
11. Whitlock Park- Tennis Courts, Walking Trail- Picnic Shelters, Swimming Pool–Lou S. Allard Drive
12. Boom Town Wing School–Tidal School Winery–only remaining building. Others are sites.
13. Gold Star School-Central Career Tech's 10 million dollar Truck Driving Training Range–Highway 99 North
14. Drumright Historical Museum (meet Drumright's fascinating story face to face.)–Harley and Broadway
15. English Gothic First United Methodist church–115 North Pennsylvania
16. Catholic Mosaic Mural "Madonna of the Streets"–South Cimarron

Sources and Bibliography

- TIGER HILL – D. Earl Newsom's Book, *Drumright, The Glory Days of a Boom Town* and *Drumright! A Thousand Memories.* (Photograph Courtesy author's files.)

- THE HUMP – Ibid.

- BOOM TOWN HOUSES – Personal interviews by Author. (Photograph Courtesy Ben Russell Collection.)

- DRUMRIGHT NEEDED A LIBRARY – Ibid. (Photograph Courtesy Author's files.)

- OLD CROW BRIDGE – Ibid. (Photograph Courtesy Ben Russell Collection.)

- METHODISTS BUILD THEIR CHURCH – Records Courtesy First United Methodist Church, Drumright. (Photograph Courtesy Ben Russell Collection.)

- VIDA WAY – Personal interviews by Author. (Photograph Courtesy Ben Russell Collection.)

- FIRST HIGH SCHOOL – Drumright High School records and personal interviews. (Photograph Courtesy Ben Russell Collection.)

- DRUMRIGHT GETS IT'S OWN BANK – Personal interviews by Author. (Photograph Courtesy Ben Russell Collection.)

- HISTORIC ROBERTS HOTEL AND TOWER THEATER – Author's files. (Photograph Courtesy Robert & Majorie Peden.)

- LODGES WERE THE SOCIAL LIFE – Ibid. (Photograph Courtesy Ben Russell Collection.)

- A SATURDAY NIGHT TOWN – Ibid. (Photograph Courtesy Ben Russell Collection.)

- THE RAILROAD STATION – Personal interview with Emma E. Akin, founder of Drumright Museum and Historical Society. (Photograph Courtesy Drumright Historical Museum.)

- AARON DRUMRIGHT HOME – Author's interview with Keith Kahle. (Photograph Author's files.)

- WAY PARK AMPHITHEATER – Author's files. (Photograph Author's files.)

- CATHOLIC CHURCH AND MOSAIC MADONNA – Ibid. (Photograph Courtesy Darla Glimp Graves.)

- FAMILY LIVING – Ibid. (Photograph Courtesy Ben Russell Collection.)

- TALENT AND CULTURE – Ibid. (Photograph Courtesy Drumright Historical Museum.)

- JEANETTE, THE TALKING PARROT – Author's files and interview with Inez Chastain. (Photograph Courtesy Drumright Historical Museum.)

- CABLE TOOL RIG – Author's files. (Photograph Courtesy Ben Russell Collection.)

- TOUR HISTORIC BOOMTOWN – (with map and addresses)